Fifty ★ *Years*

JOFFREY
BALLET

AN AMERICAN CLASSIC

"FROM OUR VERY BEGINNINGS in 1956, when
six dedicated young dancers began a cross-country
tour of one-night stands in a borrowed station wagon
to the present company, the dancers have always
been the living heart of The Joffrey. So many
of these artists have given their best performing years
to the company that, in keeping with our all-star,
no-star policy, I will single none of them out for special
thanks, though their skills have breathed the life of
their uniquely individual personalities into our varied
repertory. To all of them, and to Gerald Arpino,
my Associate Director, and one of the
original members of the company,
I owe my deepest gratitude."

— Robert Joffrey, 1981

Robert Joffrey (right top)
Gerald Arpino (right bottom)

2

1950s

IN THE FALL OF 1956, six ballet dancers hitched a U-haul to a borrowed station wagon and left New York's Greenwich Village for a tour that took them to over twenty small towns across the country. Little did they know that fifty years later their ensemble would become one of the world's premier dance companies — The Joffrey Ballet.

This small ensemble immediately began to attract attention for their focus, dedication and youthful zeal. They were able to perform in places that other larger companies could not. From community halls to churches, high school cafeterias to small theaters, the company began to forge a relationship with America's heartland, one that would come to define them later.

On the night of January 22, 1957, in the midst of a full-scale Chicago snowstorm, the Robert Joffrey Theatre Dancers opened for its first performance in a major city at Chicago's 8th Street Theatre. The critics were blown away. It was on the strength of these reviews that the company was able to secure significant tour dates and The Joffrey Ballet was truly born.

The intimacy of the company made ballet accessible to the masses. Joffrey's own PAS DES DÉESSES became the troupe's most popular work, epitomizing ballet in the public's mind with its romance, grace and athleticism.

In 1957, Joffrey added three dancers to the newly-titled Robert Joffrey Theatre Ballet. In 1959, the company expanded its touring to include more than 60 stops across the country. By bringing ballet to communities that had never seen it before, The Joffrey established itself as the "Johnny Appleseed" of dance.

JOFFREY PREMIERES

A LA GERSHWIN

LE BAL MASQUÉ

LE BAL

CONTRETEMPS

GISELLE: PEASANT PAS DE DEUX

HARPSICHORD CONCERTO

KALEIDOSCOPE

THE NUTCRACKER PAS DE DEUX

PAS DES DÉESSES

PASTORALE

PERSEPHONE

PIERROT LUNAIRE

SCARAMOUCHE

SOIRÉES MUSICALES

UMPATEEDLE

WHIRLIGIG

WITHIN FOUR WALLS

WORK OUT

YESTERDAY'S PAPERS

THE ORIGINAL COMPANY
Dancers – (clockwise from top)
Glen Tetley, Dianne Consoer,
Gerald Arpino (Co-Founder),
Brunilda Ruiz, Robert Joffrey
(Co-Founder), John Wilson and,
center, Beatrice Tompkins
Photography – Zachary Freyman

Co-Founders
Robert Joffrey &
Gerald Arpino
Photography – Unknown

PAS DES DÉESSES
The Dance of the Goddesses
(opposite page)
Choreography –
Robert Joffrey
Music – John Field
Dancers – Brunilda Ruiz,
Glen Tetley, Francoise
Martinet and Marie Paquet
Photography – Unknown

This ballet, based on an early
19th century lithograph of
the same name, depicts the
gentle rivalry between these
three real-life ballerinas as
they vie for the affections
of a Danseur Nobel.

WITHIN FOUR WALLS
(opposite page)
Choreography – Robert Joffrey
Music – John Wilson, based on Stephen Foster
Dancers – Ensemble (Gerald Arpino, second from left)
Photography – Zachary Freyman

PAS DES DÉESSES
The Dance of the Goddesses
(left)
Choreography - Robert Joffrey
Music – John Field
Dancer – Lillian Wellein
Photography – Jack Mitchell

GISELLE: PEASANT PAS DE DEUX
Choreography – Nicholas Serheyev
Music – Friedrich Burqmüller
Dancers – Paul Sutherland and Francoise Martinet
Photography – Zachary Freyman

LE BAL MASQUÉ
Choreography – Robert Joffrey
Music – Francis Poulenc
Dancers – Gerald Arpino and
Beatrice Tompkins
Photography – Zachary Freyman

(opposite page, left)
Dancers – Beatrice Tompkins and
Jonathan Watts
Photography – Zachary Freyman

PAS DE DIX
Raymonda Variations
(opposite page, top)
Choreography – George Balanchine
Music – Alexander Glazanov
Dancers – Rochelle Zide and
Gerald Arpino
Photography – Unknown

WHIRLIGIG
(opposite page, bottom)
Choreography – Todd Bolendar
Music – Wolfgang Mozart
Dancers – Marie Paquet and
Nels Jorgensen
Photography – Unknown

UMPATEEDLE
Choreography – Robert Joffrey
Music – Johann Strauss
Dancers – Jonathan Watts and Electra Arenal
Photography – Zachary Freyman

PASTORALE
Choreography – Francisco Moncion
Music – Charles Turner
Dancers – Gerald Arpino and Brunilda Ruiz
Photography – Unknown

★
Portrait of Robert Joffrey
Photography – Unknown

(below)
Robert Joffrey teaching class
at the New York High School
of Performing Arts
Photography – Unknown

13

1960s

IN 1961, THE ROBERT JOFFREY BALLET expanded to 17 dancers and embarked on a 47-city tour of America. One year later, the company again increased its size and broadened its tour destinations when the U.S. State Department sent it on an international good will tour to the Middle East, Portugal, Vienna and India. The Joffrey received rave reviews around the world for its energy and uniquely American style of blending traditional ballet with contemporary dance in ways that had not been seen before. This led to a new honor, when The Joffrey Ballet became the first American ballet company to be invited to perform in the Soviet Union.

In 1963, The Joffrey Ballet received an invitation to dance at the White House for President Kennedy. Over the years, three more invitations to perform at the White House would follow. By the mid-1960s, the company made its television debut with a performance on "The Ed Sullivan Show."

The 1960s, however, was also a time of social upheaval. The civil rights movement and the dream of "The Great Society" became eclipsed by the assassination of the Kennedy brothers and Dr. Martin Luther King. Psychedelic art, rock and roll, flower power, and the escalation of the war in Vietnam were in the headlines.

The Joffrey Ballet became emblematic of the decade, with works like Anna Soklow's *OPUS 65* which depicted dancers as defiant, barefoot hippies; Kurt Jooss' anti-war masterpiece *THE GREEN TABLE*; as well as Gerald Arpino's anti-nuclear statement *THE CLOWNS* made The Joffrey a voice of the counterculture. By 1968, Robert Joffrey's own multi-media rock ballet *ASTARTE* would grace the cover of "Time" magazine, further moving the company into the public consciousness.

JOFFREY PREMIERES

ALLEGRO BRILLANTE	*LA FILLE MAL GARDÉE (Nault)*	*PARTITA FOR 4*
ANIMUS	*FLOWER FESTIVAL IN GENZANO*	*PAS DE DEUX*
ARCS AND ANGELS		*PAS DE DIX (RAYMONDA VARIATIONS)*
ASTARTE	*THE GAME OF NOAH*	
BAGATELLES	*GAMELAN*	*PATTERNS*
BOXES	*THE GLASS HEART*	*THE POPPET*
CAKEWALK	*THE GREEN TABLE*	*QUARTET*
CAPRICES	*THE HEART OF THE MATTER*	*ROOMS*
CELLO CONCERTO	*INCUBUS*	*ROPES*
CHARIVARI	*INVITATIONS*	*ROUNDABOUT*
CLARISSA	*JAZZ*	*SCOTCH SYMPHONY*
THE CLOWNS	*JINX*	*SEA SHADOW*
CON AMORE	*KONSERVATORIET*	*SECRET PLACES*
CONTRASTS	*THE LESSON*	*SQUARE DANCE*
DIFFERENCES	*A LIGHT FANTASTIC*	*THESE THREE*
DISTRACTIONS	*THE MANNEQUINS*	*TIME OUT OF MIND*
DONIZETTI VARIATIONS	*MINKUS PAS DE TROIS*	*LE TRICORNE*
DREAMS OF GLORY	*MONCAYO 1*	*VITALITAS*
ELEGY	*MOVES*	*VIVA VIVALDI !*
FAÇADE	*NIGHTWINGS*	*WILLIAM TELL VARIATIONS*
FANFARITA	*OLYMPICS*	
FEAST OF ASHES	*OPUS 65*	
	THE PALACE	

MARCH 15, 1968

FIFTY CENTS

TIME

JOFFREY BALLET'S "ASTARTE"

★
Robert Joffrey's groundbreaking multi-media ballet *ASTARTE* appeared on the cover of *Time* magazine. This image, created by Herbert Migdoll, features Trinette Singleton and Maximiliano Zomosa.

Robert Joffrey (bottom center) and the company at the ribbon-cutting ceremony for the opening of The American Ballet Center (home of The Joffrey Ballet School) in Greenwich Village.

Photography – Jack Mitchell

(left)
Gerald Arpino and Robert Joffrey in the window of The American Ballet Center.

General Manager Alexander Ewing, Robert Joffrey and Gerald Arpino take a bow after their first season at City Center in New York City.

VIVA VIVALDI !
Choreography – Gerald Arpino
Music – Antonio Vivaldi
Dancers – Ensemble

Gerald Arpino's Spanish flavored *VIVA VIVALDI !*
is performed at the White House in 1969. The
Joffrey Ballet has appeared at the White House
four times, performing a ballet by Gerald Arpino
each time.

SECRET PLACES
Choreography – Gerald Arpino
Music – Wolfgang Mozart
Dancers – Gay Wallstrom and Dennis Wayne

Dancers on the lawn of Wolftrap
Theater in Wolftrap, VA.

★

TIME CYCLE
Choreography – Todd Bolender
Music – Lukas Foss
Dancers – Ensemble

OLYMPICS
Choreography - Gerald Arpino
Music - Toshiro Mayazumi
Dancer - Luis Fuente

MINKUS PAS DE TROIS

Choreography – George Balanchine

Music – Leon Minkus

Dancers (above) – Zelma Bustillo, Luis Fuente
and Pamara Perry

Dancers (right) – Luis Fuente and Susan Magno

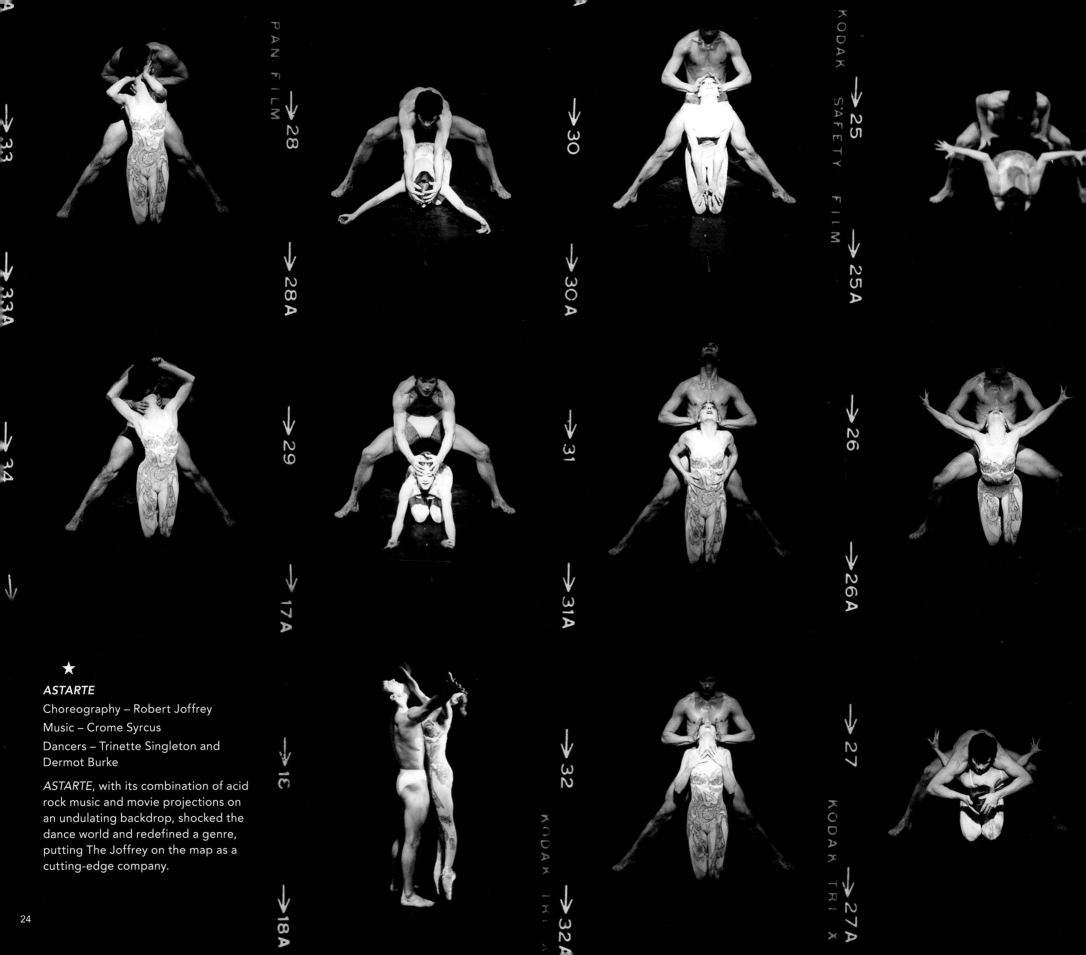

★

ASTARTE

Choreography – Robert Joffrey
Music – Crome Syrcus
Dancers – Trinette Singleton and
Dermot Burke

ASTARTE, with its combination of acid rock music and movie projections on an undulating backdrop, shocked the dance world and redefined a genre, putting The Joffrey on the map as a cutting-edge company.

★

GAMELAN

Choreography – Robert Joffrey
Music – Lou Harrison
Dancers (left) – Lisa Bradley and Michael Uthoff
Dancers (middle) – Robert Joffrey coaching Paul Sutherland

GAMELAN based on Haiku poetry, represents a fusion of Eastern and Western cultures.

★

ROOMS

Choreography – Anna Sokolow
Music – Kenyon Hopkins
Dancers – Ensemble

ROOMS is one of the earliest and most extreme modern works The Joffrey performed.

★

THE CLOWNS
(opposite page)
Choreography – Gerald Arpino
Music – Hershy Kay
Dancer – Robert Blankshine

Gerald Arpino shocked audiences and critics alike in 1968 with this allegory on nuclear holocaust. *THE CLOWNS* used ever-changing and growing plastic inflatable sculptures as props and is widely considered a 20th century masterpiece.

INCUBUS
Choreography – Gerald Arpino
Music – Anton Webern
Dancers – Lisa Bradley and Robert Blankshine
Photographer – James Howell

Taken from a monitor at the taping of the "Ed Sullivan Show" in 1966, this photo depicts dancers in Gerald Arpino's psychological study of a young girl.

FLOWER FESTIVAL IN GENZANO

Choreography – August Bournonville
Music – Edward Helsted and Holger Simon Pauli
Dancers – Lawrence Rhodes and Lone Isaksen

The Joffrey became the first American company to present the works of this renowned Danish choreographer with the performance of this ballet.

SEA SHADOW

Choreography – Gerald Arpino
Music – Maurice Ravel
Dancers – Lisa Bradley and Paul Sutherland

SEA SHADOW is one of Gerald Arpino's earliest creations and remains one of his loveliest and most popular.

FAÇADE

Choreography – Sir Frederick Ashton
Music – William Walton
Dancers – Ensemble

FAÇADE was the first ballet by Sir Fredrick Ashton,
England's preeminent choreographer ever presented
by The Joffrey. By the early 1980s, The Joffrey would have
one of the world's largest repertoires of "Sir Fred's" work.

Rehearsals at the American Ballet Center.
Dancers – Brunilda Ruiz, Gerald Arpino
and Paul Sutherland
Photographer – Ra Cantu

PAS DES DÉESSES
The Dance of the Goddesses
Choreography – Robert Joffrey
Music – John Field
Dancer (above) – Noël Mason
Dancer (right) – Charthel Arthur

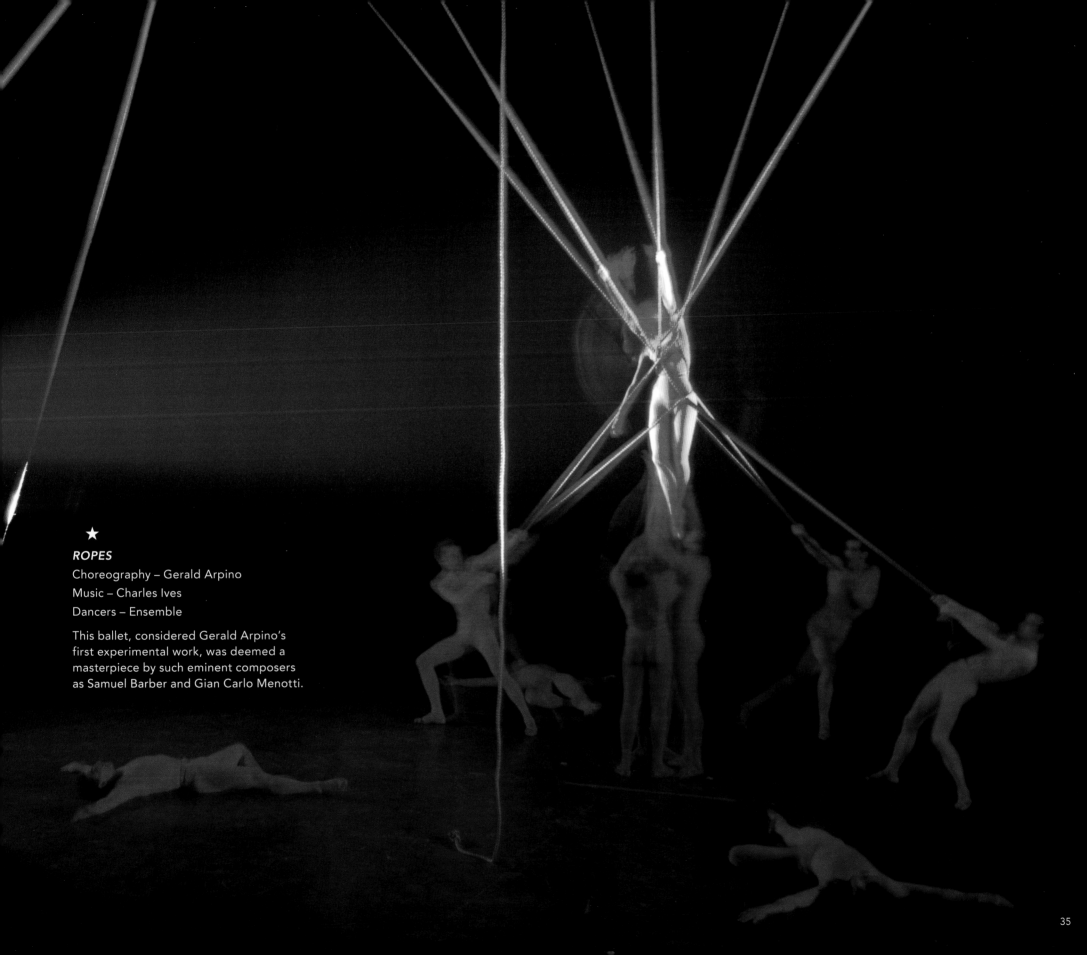

★

ROPES

Choreography – Gerald Arpino
Music – Charles Ives
Dancers – Ensemble

This ballet, considered Gerald Arpino's
first experimental work, was deemed a
masterpiece by such eminent composers
as Samuel Barber and Gian Carlo Menotti.

1970s

THE JOFFREY BALLET came into its own in the 1970s by expanding its repertoire of both classical and cutting-edge works, as well as increasing its depth of talent. Ballets like Gerald Arpino's *TRINITY* and *SACRED GROVE ON MOUNT TAMALPAIS*, with their rock scores and energetic choreography, celebrated the youth movement. Robert Joffrey broke new ground when he commissioned young choreographer Twyla Tharp to create new pieces for his dancers. *DEUCE COUPE*, set to the music of The Beach Boys, and *AS TIME GOES BY* revolutionized ballet choreography in a manner that would alter the way many choreographers approached their work.

But Robert Joffrey did not want to become defined by the times — he wanted to shape them artistically. And for this, he turned to the past. The early 20th century had been equally tumultuous and rich as the 1970s, and the avant-garde ballets of that period still had something to say to contemporary audiences. Focusing primarily on the ballets of Diaghilev's Ballet Russes, Joffrey brought the company to the attention of the art world with revivals and reconstructions of works that until then had been considered lost.

The company's profile was now clear: versatility. On any given evening, a Joffrey audience would be treated to a program featuring a rare piece of history, a cutting-edge contemporary work, a ballet of great classical refinement and a joyous dance celebrating the youth of the day. The Joffrey had become expertly diverse. And with its continued national and international touring, The Joffrey succeeded in challenging and expanding the world's concept of what an American ballet company could achieve.

JOFFREY PREMIERES

ABYSS

AFTER EDEN

L'AIR D'ESPRIT

L'APRÉS-MIDI D'UN FAUNE

AS TIME GOES BY

A BALL IN OLD VIENNA

LE BEAU DANUBE

THE BIG CITY

A BRIDEGROOM CALLED DEATH

BROUILLARDS

CACKLIN' HEN

CHABRIESQUE

CHOPIN PRELUDES

CHOURA

CON AMOR

CONFETTI

DEUCE COUPE

DEUCE COUPE II

THE DREAM

DRUMS, DREAMS, AND BANJOS

EPODE

EVENING DIALOGUES

FACE DANCERS

FIVE DANCES

GRAND PAS ESPAGNOL

HAPPILY EVER AFTER

HEPTAGON

INTERPLAY

JACKPOT

JAZZ CALENDAR

JEU DE CARTES

JIVE

KETTENTANZ

MEADOWLARK

THE MINGUS DANCES

MIRAGE

MONOTONES I

MONOTONES II

MOOR'S PAVANE

N.Y. EXPORT: OPUS JAZZ

OFFENBACH IN THE UNDERWORLD

OPUS 1

ORPHEUS TIMES LIGHT

PARADE

PAS DE DEUX HOLBERG

LES PATINEURS

PAVANE ON THE DEATH OF AN INFANTA

PETROUCHKA

PINAPPLE POLL

PULCINELLA

REFLECTIONS

THE RELATIVITY OF ICARUS

REMEMBRANCES

RODEO

ROMEO AND JULIET (Ariaz)

SACRED GROVE ON MOUNT TAMALPAIS

SOLARWIND

LE SPECTRE DE LA ROSE

THE STILL POINT

SUITE SAINT-SAËNS

TARANTELLA

TCHAIKOVSKY PAS DE DEUX

TIME CYCLE

TOUCH ME

TRINITY

VALENTINE

LA VIVANDIÈRE, PAS DE SIX

A WEDDING BOUQUET

WEEWIS

★

TRINITY
Choreography – Gerald Arpino
Music – Lee Holdridge and Alan Raph
Dancers (previous page) – Ensemble
Dancers – Christian Holder, Gary Chryst and Dermot Burke

With the premiere of *TRINITY*, The Joffrey Ballet firmly established itself as a ballet company for the counter-culture youth of the 1960s and 1970s. The backbone of this signature ballet is based on the strength and unity of three diverse characters, portrayed by the dancers to the right.

JEU DE CARTES
Choreography – John Cranko
Music – Igor Stravinsky
Dancers – Ensemble

Each section of this unique ballet plays out as an actual poker hand with the dancers representing different cards.

THE CLOWNS
(opposite page)
Choreography – Gerald Arpino
Music – Hershy Kay
Dancers – Ensemble

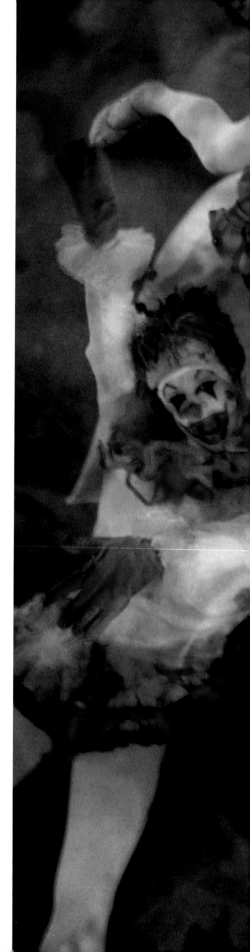

★

LES PATINEURS
The Ice Skaters
Choreographer – Sir Frederick Ashton
Music – Giaccomo Mayerbeer
Dancer – Mark Goldweber

★

FANFARITA
Choreography – Gerald Arpino
Music – Ruperto Chapi
Dancer – Ann Marie DeAngelo

N.Y. EXPORT: OPUS JAZZ
(left)
Choreography – Jerome Robbins
Music – Robert Prince
Dancers – Ensemble

CONFETTI
Choreographer – Gerald Arpino
Music – Gioacchino Rossini
Dancers – Glenn White, Sue Loyd and William Whitener

DEUCE COUPE
(opposite page)
Choreography – Twyla Tharp
Music – The Beach Boys
Dancer – Twyla Tharp

This revolutionary work was a collaboration between Twyla Tharp's modern company and The Joffrey Ballet and featured live graffiti artists on stage. *DEUCE COUPE* turned the dance world on its head and exposed Ms. Tharp's work to greater audiences.

MOVES
Choreography – Jerome Robbins
Music – None
Dancers – Ensemble

In 1967, The Joffrey Ballet became the first company other than Jerome Robbins' own Ballets USA to perform this work in 1967. *MOVES* is danced in total silence, requiring complete concentration from both the dancers and the audience. Mr. Robbins called his *MOVES*, "a lesson in audience behavior."

★

THE RELATIVITY OF ICARUS
(opposite page)
Choreography – Gerald Arpino
Music – Gethard Samuel
Dancers – Ted Nelson and Russell Sultzbach

ASTARTE
(right)
Choreography – Robert Joffrey
Music – Chrome Syrcus
Dancers – Nancy Robinson and Christian Holder

47

THE GREEN TABLE

Choreography – Kurt Jooss
Music – Frederick Cohen
Dancers – Ensemble

The Joffrey became the first American company to present
this great anti-war ballet choreographed in Germany in 1932.
THE GREEN TABLE became a signature work for The Joffrey
in the 1960s and 1970s and performances of this ballet helped
establish the company's reputation as a leader in presenting
socially relevant works.

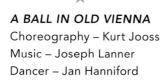

A BALL IN OLD VIENNA
Choreography – Kurt Jooss
Music – Joseph Lanner
Dancer – Jan Hanniford

THE BIG CITY
Choreography – Kurt Jooss
Music – Alexandre Tansman
Dancer – Charthel Arthur

PAVANE ON THE DEATH OF AN INFANTA
Choreography – Kurt Jooss
Music – Maurice Ravel
Dancer – Francesca Corkle

★

PETROUCHKA

Choreography – Michel Fokine
Music – Igor Stravinsky
Dancer – Gary Chryst
Dancers (opposite page) – Ensemble

Rudolf Nureyev danced the role of *PETROUCHKA* in this production and can be seen (in costume, in center) taking a bow with the company following a performance on Broadway at the Mark Hellinger Theater.

PARADE

Choreography – Leonide Massine
Music – Erik Satie
Dancers – Janey Kawagucki and Russell Sultzbach

PARADE is a 1917 collaboration conceived by Jean Cocteau, sets and costumes designed by Pablo Picasso. The Joffrey made history in 1973 when this ballet became the first reconstruction of the great lost works of the Diaghilev era.

PARADE

Choreography – Leonide Massine
Music – Erik Satie
Dancers (top) – Ensemble as
Picasso's Managers.
Dancer (bottom left) – Gary Chryst
Dancer (bottom right) –
Gary Chryst

This collection of photos reflects
the visual artistry of Pablo Picasso's
innovative designs as displayed by
the costumes of The Acrobats
(opposite page), The Managers (top)
and the Chinese Conjurer (bottom
right). Picasso paid close attention
to all the visual details of this piece,
including the dancers' make-up.
Leonide Massine is seen applying
Gary Chryst's make-up for the premiere telecast of the PBS series
"Dance in America," while Claude
Picasso, the artist's son, takes a
photograph (bottom left).

AFTER EDEN
Choreography – John Butler
Music – Lee Hoiby
Dancers – Starr Danias and Dennis Wayne

SACRED GROVE ON MOUNT TAMALPAIS
Choreography – Gerald Arpino
Music – Alan Raph
Dancers – Starr Danias and Dennis Wayne

RODEO
Choreography – Agnes DeMille
Music – Aaron Copeland
Dancers – Ensemble

REMEMBRANCES
Choreography – Robert Joffrey
Music – Richard Wagner
Dancer – Francesca Corkle
Dancers (opposite page) –
Charthel Arthur and Robert Thomas
rehearse with Robert Joffrey and
Scott Barnard (Ballet Master)

REMEMBRANCES was danced
as a part of the inaugural "Dance
in America" program for PBS.
The photograph on the opposite
page depicts Robert Joffrey
choreographing this signature piece.

★

This study of dancers Burton Taylor (standing) and Russell Sultzbach, dressed as characters Oberon and Puck from William Shakespeare's comedic play "A Midsummer Night's Dream," was taken in the lush forests of Wolftrap, Virginia. The Joffrey became the inaugural company of the Wolftrap Theater with their performance of *THE DREAM*.

THE DREAM

Choreography – Sir Frederick Ashton

Music – Felix Mendelssohn

Dancer (opposite page, left) –
Russell Sultzbach

Dancers (left) – Burton Taylor
and Rebecca Wright

Dancer (right) – Rebecca Wright

The Joffrey became the first company outside of England's Royal Ballet to perform this ballet in 1973. *THE DREAM* set a benchmark for The Joffrey Ballet as it was the largest production of classical ballet The Joffrey had ever performed.

1980s

THE 1980S SAW EVEN MORE reconstructions and grander large-scale productions for The Joffrey. In 1981, the company premiered its full-length production of John Cranko's *THE TAMING OF THE SHREW*. It soon followed with his lavish *ROMEO AND JULIET* in 1984 and the even more ambitious *LA FILLE MAL GARDÉE* by Sir Frederick Ashton in 1986.

While continuing to be based at New York's City Center, The Joffrey became bicoastal in 1983 when it was invited to become the resident ballet company of the Los Angeles Music Center. This ground-breaking ten-year arrangement created a model that was adopted by several other American ballet companies.

In 1987, The Joffrey produced two seminal ballets in partnership with the University of Iowa Foundation/Hancher Auditorium in Iowa City, Iowa. The first, a reconstruction of Nijinksy's 1913 *LE SACRE DU PRINTEMPS*, became a major world event. The second, *THE NUTCRACKER*, established The Joffrey Ballet's interpretation as a holiday classic. This was Robert Joffrey's last production. At the world premiere of *THE NUTCRACKER* in December 1987, Robert Joffrey took his final bow. In March of the following year, while performing Ashton's *THE DREAM* in Chicago, the company received word that Mr. Joffrey had passed away.

In 1988, Gerald Arpino became Artistic Director of The Joffrey Ballet.

JOFFREY PREMIERES

ALTERED STATES	LIGHT RAIN
ANNIVERSARY PAS DE DEUX	LOVE SONGS
ARDEN COURT	MO MIX BEA BOP
BILLY THE KID	MOMENTUM
BIRTHDAY VARIATIONS	MYTHICAL HUNTERS
CELEBRATION	NIGHT
CLOVEN KINGDOM	LES NOCES
CONCERTO GROSSO	THE NUTCRACKER
COTILLON	PASSAGE
DIVERDISSEMENTE	POSTCARDS
DREAM DANCES	QUARTER TONES FOR MR. B
ESTEEMED GUESTS	RANDOM DANCES
LA FILLE MAL GARDÉE (Ashton)	RELÂCHE
FIRE	RETURN TO A STRANGE LAND
FIVE BRAHMS WALTZES IN THE MANNER OF ISADORA DUNCAN	ROMEO AND JULIET (Cranko)
FORCE FIELD	ROUND OF ANGELS
FORGOTTEN LAND	LA SACRE DU PRINTEMPS
THE GARDENS OF BOBOLI	SQUARE DEAL
HELENA	THE TAMING OF THE SHREW
HEXAMERON	THREE PRELUDES
ILLUMINATIONS	TWO-A-DAY
ISADORA	UNFOLDING
ITALIAN SUITE	UNTITLED
JAMBOREE	

★

TOUCH ME
Choreography – Gerald Arpino
Music –
Reverend James Cleveland
Dancer – Edward Morgan

★

LE SACRE DU PRINTEMPS
Choreography – Vaslav Nijinsky
Music – Igor Stravinsky
Dancer – Beatrize Rodriguez
Dancers (previous page) –
Ensemble

The original 1913 choreography for
this ballet was researched and recon-
structed for more than ten years by
dance historian Millicent Hodson,
while the original sets and costumes
were meticulously researched and
recreated by Kenneth Archer. The
photo on the previous page is from
the 1988 production for the PBS
series "Dance in America." Note the
hand-painted floor that was crafted

★

CELEBRATION
Choreography – Gerald Arpino
Music – Dmitri Shostakovitch
Dancers – Cameron Basden

ILLUMINATIONS

Choreography – Sir Frederick Ashton

Music – Benjamin Britten

Dancer (left) – Patricia Miller

Dancer – Beatriz Rodriguez

The Joffrey became the first company outside of the New York City Ballet to perform this 1950 masterpiece in 1980.

★

FIRE

Choreography – Laura Dean
Music – Laura Dean
Dancers – Patricia Brown and
Luis Perez

The extraordinary backdrop and the
costumes for this ballet were created
by Chicago architect Michael Graves.

CLOVEN KINGDOM
Choreography – Paul Taylor
Music – Acangelo Corelli,
Henry Cowell and Malloy Miller
Dancer – Julie Janus

67

★

LIGHT RAIN

Choreography – Gerald Arpino
Music – Douglas Adams and Russ Gauthier
Dancers (left) – Ensemble with Gerald Arpino

Gerald Arpino's sensuous and exotic ballet has strong
eastern influences and has become one of his most
popular and enduring signature works.

★

TRINITY
Choreography – Gerald Arpino
Music – Lee Holdridge and Alan Raph
Dancer (left) – Edward Stierle
Dancer (right) – Mark Goldweber

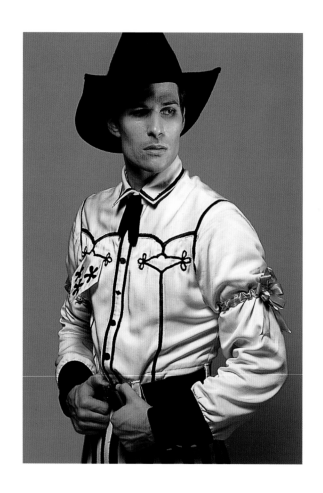  

BILLY THE KID

Choreography – Eugene Loring
Music – Aaron Copland
Dancers (left to right) – Douglas Martin,
Jerel Hilding and Tom Mossbrucker.

70

BIRTHDAY VARIATIONS
Choreography – Gerald Arpino
Music – Giuseppi Verdi
Dancers – Ensemble

This ballet was commissioned as a birthday gift to long-time Joffrey friend and supporter, Chicagoan Becky D'Angelo.

★
ROMEO AND JULIET
Choreography – John Cranko
Music – Serge Prokofiev
Dancers – Ensemble from the
2003 revival in Chicago
Dancers – Dawn Caccamo and
Glenn Edgerton

The Joffrey became the first
American Ballet Company to present
this full-length masterpiece in 1984.
The exquisite costumes, designed
by Jurgen Rose, are made from fine
raw silks and leather.

RODEO
Choreographer – Agnes DeMille
Music – Aaron Copland
Dancer – Carole Valleskey

LA FILLE MAL GARDÉE
Choreography – Sir Frederick Ashton
Music – Ferdinand Herold
Dancers – Ensemble

LA FILLE MAL GARDÉE, with its colorful maypole, became the fourth and largest full-length ballet The Joffrey had yet staged.

ITALIAN SUITE

Choreography – Gerald Arpino
Music – Ermanno Wolf-Ferrari
Dancers – James Canfield and
Patricia Miller

L'APRÈS MIDI D'UN FAUNE
Choreography – Vaslav Nijinsky
Music – Claude Debussy
Dancer – Tyler Walters (opposite page)
Dancers – Charlene Gehm (center) with Ensemble

 ★

POSTCARDS
Choreography – Robert Joffrey
Music – Erik Satie
Dancers (left) – Denise Jackson
and Ross Stretton

★

KETTENTANZ
Choreography – Gerald Arpino
Music – Johann Strauss and
Johann Simon Mayer
Dancer – Deborah Dawn

★
LES NOCES
Choreography – Bronislava Nijinska
Music – Igor Stravinsky
Dancers – Ensemble

★

RELÂCHE

Choreography – Moses Pendleton
Music – Erik Satie
Dancer (opposite page) – Starr Danias
Dancers – Starr Danias and
Gregory Huffman

PETROUCHKA

Choreography – Michel Fokine

Music – Igor Stravinsky

Dancers – Ensemble with Robert Joffrey

Dancers (right) – Ensemble with Rudolf Nureyev (center as Petrouchka)

Robert Joffrey (above) discusses some fine points with dancer/ballet mistress Diane Orio during the PBS filming of *PETROUCHKA* for "Dance in America" in 1980. Rudolf Nureyev was a guest artist and performed the lead role with the company for this production.

THE NUTCRACKER

Choreography – Gerald Arpino, Scott Barnard
and George Verdak

Music – Peter Tchaikovsky

Dancer - Kim Sagami

Puppeteer (opposite page) – Francis Kane

Robert Joffrey's production of *THE NUTCRACKER*
features beautifully intricate new sections of
choreography by Gerald Arpino. Mr. Arpino's
Snow Scene and *Waltz of the Flowers* are audience
favorites. The extraordinary flower costumes shown
on these pages, as well as all other costumes for
this ballet, were designed by John David Ridge.

The Joffrey's annual production of this
timeless holiday classic utilizes approximately
120 local children to portray 60 different roles,
including the Polichenelles (as seen on the
opposite page with puppet Mother Ginger).

★

THE GREEN TABLE
(left)
Choreography – Kurt Jooss
Music – Frederick Cohen
Dancer – Philip Jerry

NIGHT
(above)
Choreography – Laura Dean
Music – Laura Dean
Dancers – Lynne Chervony Belsky and Glenn Edgerton

NIGHT is the first piece Laura Dean created for a ballet company, both choreographing and writing the music, she also wrote the music. Ms. Dean went on to create eight works for The Joffrey Ballet.

THE HEART OF THE MATTER
Choreography – James Kudelka
Music – Serge Prokofiev
Dancers – Ensemble

This moving ballet is based on a poem by Dorothy Parker.

1990s

WITH ROBERT JOFFREY'S PASSING, Gerald Arpino faced the triple challenge of staying true to the company's roots, moving that vision forward in a way that would appeal to the "music television" generation, and dealing with the abrupt and dramatic changes in arts funding that all performing institutions faced in America during the 1990s.

Continuing Robert Joffrey's passion for restoring the great ballets of the early 20th century, Gerald Arpino acquired Leonide Massine's 1933 *LES PRÉSAGES* in 1992. This acquisition brought further recognition of The Joffrey as both a reconstructor of lost works and a repository of modern masterpieces.

In 1993, The Joffrey mounted *BILLBOARDS*, a full-length work comprised of four sections created by different choreographers. Set to the music of rock musician Prince, *BILLBOARDS* attracted new and younger audiences to ballet and created a sensation that took the company around the world several times over. Later filmed for PBS' "Dance in America" series, *BILLBOARDS* sustained The Joffrey during a financially precarious period.

By the mid-1990s, the company determined it was time to make a strategic change. Rather than stay in New York City, where competition for the funding dollar was fierce, The Joffrey decided to relocate to a major city that did not already have an internationally renowned ballet company. Known as the quintessential American city, Chicago seemed the obvious choice. Chicago was home to some of the company's greatest supporters and a mainstay of the company's touring schedule. Fittingly, Chicago had also been The Joffrey's first major tour stop some 40 years earlier. Thus in 1995, The Joffrey Ballet moved to Chicago.

JOFFREY PREMIERES

AFFECTION	*PRAYER*
AFTER THE FALL	*LES PRÈSAGES*
BILLBOARDS	*RUNAWAY TRAIN*
CANTE	*SPRING WATERS*
CAUGHT	*STRUCTURE*
CLOSURE	*TENSILE INVOLVEMENT*
COPLAND MOTETS	*A TRI-FLING*
CREATIVE FORCE	
EMPYREAN DANCES	
FOOTNOTES FOR RJ	
FRANKIE & JOHNNY	
THE GARDEN OF VILLANDRY	
INITIATION	
INNER SPACE	
KALI MA	
KAY'S LILT	
LACRYMOSA	
LEGENDS	
LEGENDS II	
LIGHT FIELD	
LILA	
MOON OF THE FALLING LEAVES	
NUESTROS VALSES	
PANORAMAGRAM	

★

BILLBOARDS
Willing and Able
Choreographer – Peter Pucci
Music – Prince Rogers Nelson (Prince)
Dancers – Maia Wilkins and Pierre Lockett

Four choreographers (Laura Dean, Charles Moulton, Peter Pucci and Margo Sappington) each created different sections of this full evening of dance produced by Gerald Arpino. *BILLBOARDS* is set to four songs by pop artist Prince: *Slide, Sometimes it Snows in April, Thunder/Purple Rain* and *Willing and Able.*

★
LILA
Choreography – Alonso King
Music – Donald Ivan Fontowitz
Dancers – Beatriz Rodriguez and Brent Phillips

MOON OF THE FALLING LEAVES
(opposite page)
Choreography – Peter Pucci
Music – Brent Michael Davids
Dancers – (top to bottom) Sam Franke,
Patrick Simonello, Michael Anderson and
Pierre Lockett

MOON OF THE FALLING LEAVES is a tribute
to Native Americans with music written by a
Mohican composer.

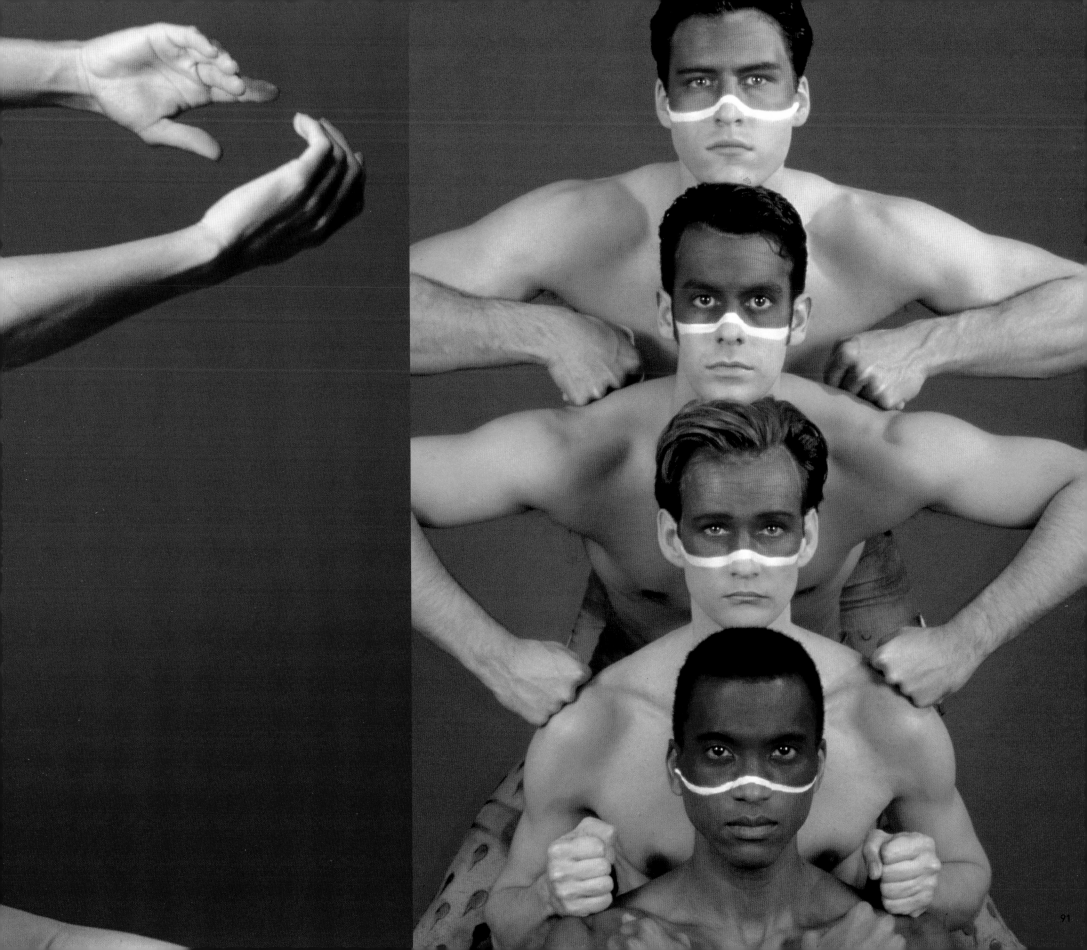

REFLECTIONS
(opposite page, left)
Choreography – Gerald Arpino
Music – Peter Tchaikovsky
Dancers – Emily Patterson and
Davis Robertson

L'AIR D'ESPRIT
(opposite page, right)
Choreography – Gerald Arpino
Music – Adolph Adam
Dancer – Maia Wilkins

Gerald Arpino choreographed this beautiful
ballet in honor of early 20th century ballerina
Olga Spessitsiva.

SUITE SAINT-SAËNS
Choreography – Gerald Arpino
Music – Camille Saint-Saëns
Dancers – Calvin Kitten and Randy Herrera

FOOTNOTES FOR RJ

Choreography – Gerald Arpino
Music – Teo Macero
Dancers – Cynthia Giannini,
Trinity Hamilton and Terace Jones

FOOTNOTES FOR RJ is
Gerald Arpino's 1998 tribute
to Robert Joffrey and his love
of the Balanchine style.

L'APRES MIDI D'UN FAUNE

Choreography – Vaslav Nijinsky
Music – Claude Debussy
Dancer – Davis Robertson

LES PRÉSAGES
Choreography – Leonide Massine
Music – Peter Tchaikovsky
Dancer (right) – Guoping Wang
Dancers (opposite page) –
Ensemble

THE GREEN TABLE
(below)
Choreography – Kurt Jooss
Music – Frederick Cohen
Dancers – Ensemble

CAUGHT
(opposite page)
Choreography – David Parsons
Music – Robert Fripp
Dancers – Taryn Kaschock,
Terace Jones and Davis Robertson

CAUGHT features a single dancer who
appears to be walking on air, thanks to
the continuous pulse of a strobe light.

CONFETTI
Choreography – Gerald Arpino
Music – Gioacchino Rossini
Dancer – Jennifer Goodman

TOUCH ME
Choreography –
Gerald Arpino
Music –
Reverend James Cleveland
Dancer – Pierre Lockett

INNER SPACE
(opposite page)
Choreography –
Mehmet Sander
Music – None
Dancers – Kim Sagami,
Todd Stickney and
John Sheaffer

Three dancers move and
manipulate themselves inside
a large Plexiglas box to the
sounds of complete silence.

★

VIVA VIVALDI !
Choreography – Gerald Arpino
Music – Antonio Vivaldi
Dancer – Lorena Feijoo

★

MONOTONES I
Choreography – Sir Frederick Ashton
Music – Erik Satie
Dancers – Calvin Kitten,
Jennifer Goodman and Davida Haas

103

★
FRANKIE AND JOHNNY
Choreography – Ruth Page (of Chicago)
Music – Jerome Moross
Dancers – Maia Wilkins as Frankie

LA VIVANDIÈRE, PAS DE SIX
Choreography – August Saint-Leon
Music – D. F. Auber
Dancers – Calvin Kitten and Leticia Oliveira

The Joffrey Ballet was the first company
to research and reconstruct this 19th
century miniature.

THE MOOR'S PAVANE
Choreography – Jose Limon
Music – Henry Purcell
Dancer – Suzanne Lopez

THE MOOR'S PAVANE is
a brilliant miniature telling
the complete story of
William Shakespeare's
tragic "Othello."

★

PANORAMAGRAM
Choreography –
Charles Moulton
Music – Bill Obrecht
Dancer – Nicole Duffy
Dancers (right) – Ensemble

LEGENDS
The Man that Got Away
(opposite page)
Choreography – Sherry Zunker Dow
Music – Judy Garland
Dancer – Julie Janus

Dance for Val
Choreography – Joanna Haigood
Music – Edith Piaf
Dancer – Maia Wilkins

LEGENDS, like *BILLBOARDS*, was a
collaboration of choreographers including
Ann Marie DeAngelo, Sherry Zunker Dow,
Joanna Haigood, Ann Reinking and Margo
Sappington. Sections were set to songs
by female pop artists Ella Fitzgerald,
Judy Garland, Lena Horne, Bette Midler,
Edith Piaf and Barbra Streisand. The photo
to the right appeared on the May 1996
cover of *Dance Magazine*.

BILLBOARDS
The closing moment of the finale.
(opposite page)

The Question of You
(above)
Choreographer – Peter Pucchi
Music – Prince Rogers Nelson (Prince)
Dancers – Jodie Gates and
Phillip Gardner

Purple Rain
(below)
Choreographer – Charles Molton
Music – Prince Rogers Nelson (Prince)
Dancer – Elizabeth Parkinson

Slide
Choreographer – Margo Sappington
Music – Prince Rogers Nelson (Prince)
Dancers – Suzanne Lopez and
Adam Sklute

THE NUTCRACKER

Choreography – Gerald Arpino,
Scott Barnard and George Verdak

Music – Peter Tchaikovsky

Dancers (both) – Ensemble

The Joffrey's NUTCRACKER production is unique in that
three physically disabled children are included in the annual
children's cast. This came to be as a result of an invitation
from Mr. Arpino at a speaking engagement for any child in
the audience to come and audition. Unexpectedly, Steven,
a wheelchair-bound child, came to the audition seeking a
part in the ballet. Mr. Arpino was so touched by the boy's
tenacity that he created a special part for him which has
remained a signature role ever since.

2000s

THE NEW MILLENNIUM BECAME a building time for The Joffrey Ballet, as it worked to secure and strengthen its new support base in Chicago. Capita anew Cranko's *THE TAMING OF THE SHREW* and *ROMEO AND JULIET*, and bringing into the repertoire new works such as Ashton's *CINDERELLA*, a final wish of the late Robert Joffrey.

In 2003, Gerald Arpino, whose existing body of work had become the backbone of the company's repertoire, began to choreograph again following a 15-year hiatus. In quick succession, Arpino successfully created the socially-relevant *I/DNA* which addressed capital punishment and *RUTH, RICORDI PER DUE*, a small masterpiece created in memory of Ruth Levy, a longtime friend and Joffrey supporter.

The new millennium also saw The Joffrey appear in two major motion pictures: "Save the Last Dance" and Robert Altman's feature film "The Company." Both movies wove stories around the challenges facing dancers and the overwhelming commitment of skill and stamina needed to succeed. This same profile is embedded in the core of today's Joffrey.

Winning consistent critical acclaim and rave reviews that produce ever-growing audiences, The Joffrey continues to secure its future as a healthy, vibrant performing arts institution in Chicago. The new Joffrey Tower, in the heart of The Loop, will provide dancers and staff a permanent home and afford fans a place to watch rehearsals and small performances.

From its humble beginnings in America's heartland to its current position as Chicago's premier ballet company, The Joffrey Ballet is truly an American Classic. Its success can be traced to the sheer will of two extraordinary men — Robert Joffrey and Gerald Arpino — whose hard work, dedication, commitment and creative inspiration have allowed it to prevail for 50 years.

JOFFREY PREMIERES

APOLLO

APPALACHIAN SPRING

CINDERELLA

CROSSING

DARK ELEGIES

I/DNA

JEUX

LAURENCIA PAS D'ACTION

LILAC GARDEN

LYRIC DISCOURSE

MIRACLE, INTERRUPTED

MOTOWN SUITES

PARTITA FOR RC

PRODIGAL SON

RUTH, RICORDI PER DUE

STRANGE PRISONERS

WHITE WIDOW

Kathleen Thielhelm and Fabrice Calmels stand in a pose based on George Balanchine's *APOLLO* in front of the sculpture "Cloud Gate" by artist Anish Kapoor, located in Chicago's Millennium Park.

THE NUTCRACKER
The Waltz of the Snowflakes
Choreography – Gerald Arpino
Music – Peter Tchaikovsky
Dancers – Ensemble

★

A WEDDING BOUQUET

Choreography – Sir Frederick Ashton

Music – Lord Berners

Dancers (both) – Ensemble

The comic *A WEDDING BOUQUET* is a farce that exposes the absurdity of aristocratic country life through the activities associated with a wedding. The ballet is highly unique to the art form as the cast features a narrator, seated on the stage, who provides commentary written by Gertrude Stein. It

was the strength of this ballet and others of The Joffrey's Ashton repertoire that brought the company back to New York and the Metropolitan Opera House for the 2004 Ashton Centennial Celebration.

raphy – Gerald Arpino

Gustav Mahler

– (center) Victoria Jaiani and

Pergande with Ensemble

THE TAMING OF THE SHREW

Choreography – John Cranko

Music – Domenico Scarlatti

Dancers – Julianne Kepley
and Willy Shives

Dancer – (right) Maia Wilkins

★

VALENTINE
Choreography – Gerald Arpino
Music – Jacob Druckman
Dancers – Fabrice Calmels and Julianne Kepley

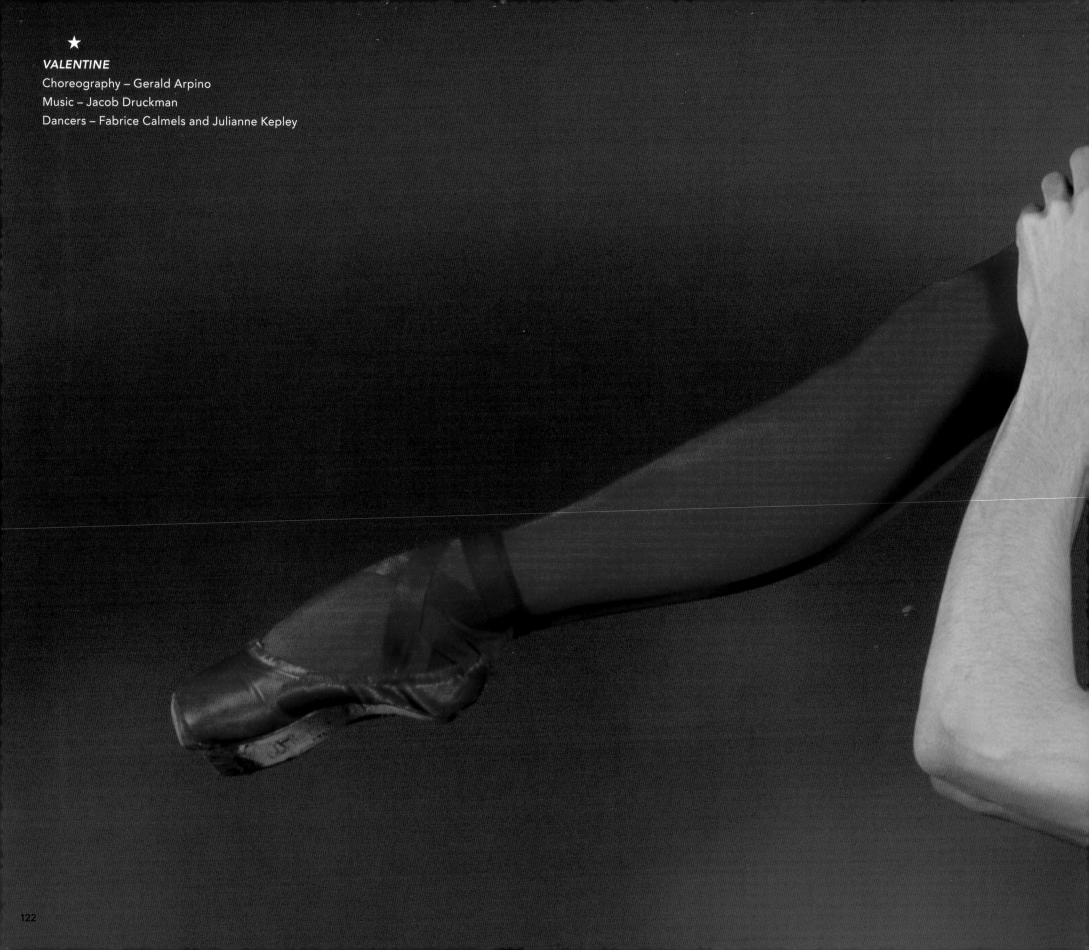

★

CELEBRATION
(left)
Choreography – Gerald Arpino
Music – Dmitri Shostakovitch
Dancers – Joanna Wozniak and
Temur Suluashvili

CREATIVE FORCE
Choreography – Laura Dean
Music – John Zeretske
Dancers – Ensemble

CREATIVE FORCE was one of the ballets
performed by The Joffrey in Robert Altman's
2003 film "The Company" starring
Neve Campbell as a promising young
dancer, James Franco as her love interest
and Malcolm McDowell as the artistic
director. Ms. Campbell, a classically trained
ballet dancer, took class daily with the
company and danced her own roles with
The Joffrey in simulated performances.

(below)
Filmmaker Robert Altman and Gerald Arpino
observe a rehearsal. (bottom)

★ Valerie Robin dressed for Arpino's
SUITE SAINT SAËNS in The Joffrey's
rehearsal studios.

THE DREAM
Choreography – Sir Frederick Ashton
Music – Felix Mendelssohn
Dancers – Ensemble
Dancers – (opposite page, above)
Maia Wilkins and Matthew Adamczyk
Dancers – (opposite page, below)
Fabrice Calmels and Julianne Kepley

★
MONOTONES II
Choreography – Sir Frederick Ashton
Music – Erik Satie
Dancer – Victoria Jaiani

★
N.Y. EXPORT: OPUS JAZZ
Choreography – Jerome Robbins
Music – Robert Prince
Dancers – Ensemble

Jerome Robbins created *N.Y. EXPORT: OPUS JAZZ* during the same time period that he created Broadway's breakthrough musical "West Side Story."

★

ASTARTE
Choreography – Robert Joffrey
Music – Crome Syrcus
Dancers – Trinity Hamilton and Domingo Rubio

(opposite page)
This montage superimposes a photo of
garden leaves over a portrait of dancer
Trinity Hamilton as Astarte, the goddess
of sex, love, war and fertility.

LIGHT RAIN
Choreography – Gerald Arpino
Music – Douglas Adams and Russ Gauthier
Dancers (opposite page) – Ensemble
Dancers – Trinity Hamilton and Sam Franke

★

APOLLO
Choreography – George Balanchine
Music – Igor Stravinsky
Dancers – Victoria Jaiani and
Fabrice Calmels
Photography – Barbara Levy Kipper

★

RUTH, RICORDI PER DUE
(left)
Choreography – Gerald Arpino
Music – Tomasso Albinoni
Dancers – Maia Wilkins and
Willy Shives
Photography – Barbara Levy Kipper

Long-time Joffrey supporter Barbara
Levy Kipper commissioned this
intimate creation from Gerald Arpino
in honor of her mother Ruth Levy.

★

CLOWNS
(above)
Choreography – Gerald Arpino
Music – Hershy Kay
Dancers – Ensemble
Photography – Barbara Levy Kipper

★
LES NOCES
(opposite page)
Choreography – Bronislava Nijinska
Music – Igor Stravinsky
Dancers – Ensemble

PETROUCHKA
Choreography – Michel Fokine
Music – Igor Stravinsky
Dancer – Willy Shives

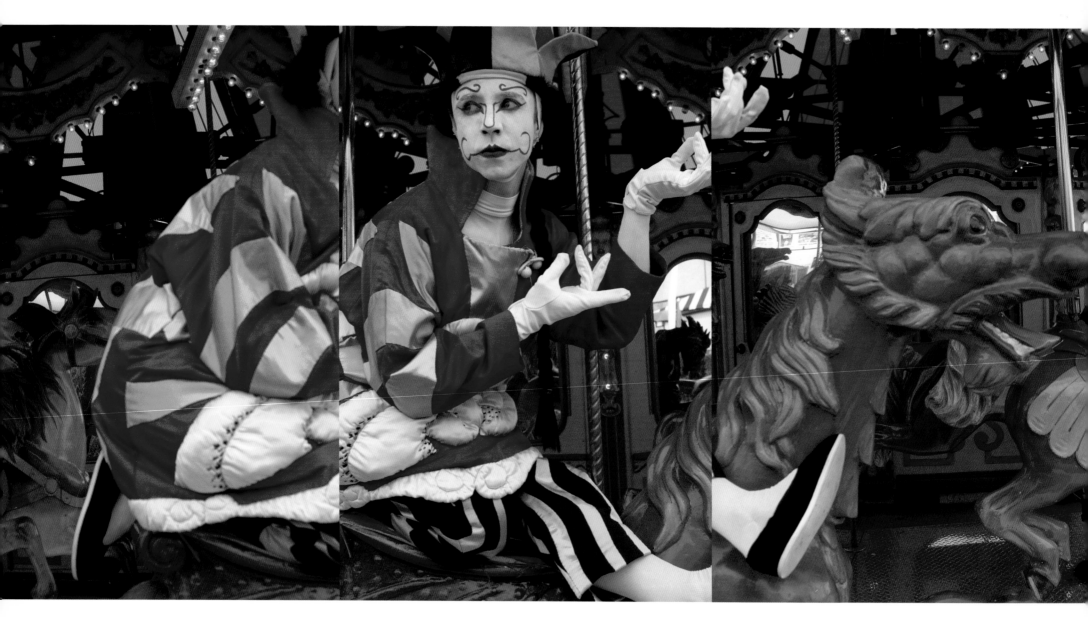

Joffrey dancers Calvin Kitten (left) posed in costume from Leonide Massine's *PARADE* and Suzanne Lopez (right) in costume from Gerald Arpino's *L'AIR D'ESPRIT* on the carousel at Navy Pier for Herbert Migdoll's 2005 exhibition, "Joffrey Carousel."

VIVA VIVALDI !
Choreographer – Gerald Arpino
Music – Antonio Vivaldi
Dancers – April Daly and Erica Lynette Edwards

BIRTHDAY VARIATIONS
Choreography – Gerald Arpino
Music – Giuseppi Verdi
Dancer – Deanne Brown

ROMEO AND JULIET
Choreography – John Cranko
Music – Serge Prokofiev
Dancer (below left) – Michael Levine
Dancer (below right) – Brian McSween

★
APPALACHIAN SPRING
Choreography – Martha Graham
Music – Aaron Copland
Dancers – Ensemble

★

APOLLO
Choreography – George Balanchine
Music – Igor Stravinsky
Dancers – Victoria Jaiani and
Fabrice Calmels with (hidden)
Kathleen Thielhelm and Valerie Robin

RETURN TO A STRANGE LAND

Choreography – Jiri Kylian

Music – Leos Janacek

Dancers – Willy Shives and Maia Wilkins

The Joffrey's performance of this haunting ballet was the first work by Jiri Kylian ever to be presented by an American company.

STRANGE PRISONERS
Choreography – Davis Robertson
Music – Johann Sebastian Bach,
Mark O'Conner and various artists
Dancers – Ensemble

I/DNA

Choreography – Gerald Arpino
Music – Charles Ives and Arnold Roth
Dancers – Ensemble

Gerald Arpino dedicated this powerful commentary regarding capital punishment to the loved ones of those men and women who have been wrongfully executed; The Center on Wrongful Convictions, Northwestern University School of Law; and to all those who fight for the lives of the innocent.

★

ROMEO AND JULIET
(left)
Choreography – John Cranko
Music – Serge Prokofiev
Dancers – Maia Wilkins and Willy Shives
Dancers (right) – John Gluckman and Willy Shives
Photography (right) – Sasha Fornari

...*SILE INVOLVEMENT* remains
...ant-garde today as it did when
...piece premiered in 1953. This
..., as well as *WHITE WIDOW*,
...red to the right, was among the
...ts presented in Robert Altman's
...ure film "The Company."

Gerald Arpino

"THE JOFFREY BALLET is imbued with the true spirit of America. Like the American people, our repertoire is a kaleidoscope of nationalities, styles and individuality. Robert Joffrey and I were two young Americans who founded this company on youthful idealism and joy. We believed in the American dream.

Through fifty years we have been watched over by angels. Angels of this earth who see us through the tough times and angels from above who guide this uniquely American vision of dance."

— *Gerald Arpino, 2006*

INDEX OF BALLETS

ACKNOWLEDGEMENTS

Special thanks to the following underwriters for their support of this publication:

The Women's Board of The Joffrey Ballet

Patti Selander Eylar and Charlie R. Gardner

Jacky and Michael Ferro

Kathleen and Dennis Klaeser

Mary Lyman

Traci and Barry Mansur

Helen Hall Melchior

Janet L. Melk

Maureen Dwyer Smith

Kim and Miles White

We thank all of The Joffrey dancers and various photographers, especially Herbert Migdoll, for allowing their images to be included in this book, as well as our committee and the staff of The Joffrey Ballet who worked tirelessly, writing and researching the photographic archives to compile and present this historic and artistic representation of a true American classic.

With great appreciation and affection,

KATHLEEN KLAESER *and* **KIM WHITE**
Co-Chairs, Women's Board Anniversary Publication Committee

| Patti Eylar | Helen Melchior | Harriet Ross |
| Barbara Levy Kipper | Kerrie Kennedy Mudd | Ann Waters |

CREDITS

This book is presented by

THE WOMEN'S BOARD OF THE JOFFREY BALLET

in celebration of The Joffrey's 50th Anniversary.

*Photography by Herbert Migdoll with additional selected photographs by
Ra Cantu, Zachary Freyman, Sasha Fornari, James Howell, Barbara Levy Kipper and Jack Mitchell.
End leaf photography by Vladimir Bliokh, Ra Cantu, Robert Carl, James Howell, Ruth Levy,
Michael Laurence, Herbert Migdoll, Jack Mitchell and unidentified sources.
TIME Magazine © 1968 Time Inc. Reprinted by permission.*

CONTRIBUTORS: *Gerald Arpino, Charthel Arthur, Cameron Basden, Jennifer A. Dettloff, Sasha Fornari, Mark Goldweber,
Amanda Golucki, Laura Iwanenko, Kathleen Klaeser, Herbert Migdoll, Kerrie Kennedy Mudd, Megan Severs,
Adam Sklute, Dorothy Suffel, Jon H. Teeuwissen and Kim White*

*Designed by Herbert Migdoll and Vieceli Design Company
Production by InnerWorkings
Manufactured in England*

Copyright 2006 by The Joffrey Ballet

ISBN 0-9748603-6-0

Additional copies of this book may be purchased by contacting

THE JOFFREY BALLET

*70 East Lake Street, Suite 1300, Chicago, Illinois 60601
312-739-0120
www.joffrey.com*

Fifty ★ *Years*

JOFFREY
BALLET

AN AMERICAN CLASSIC